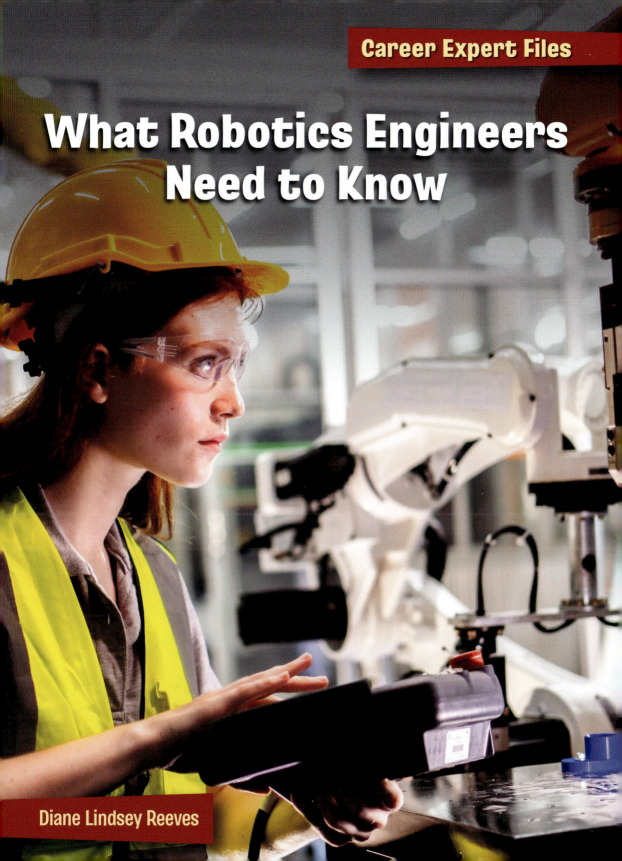

Career Expert Files

What Robotics Engineers Need to Know

Diane Lindsey Reeves

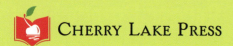

Published in the United States of America by Cherry Lake Publishing Group
Ann Arbor, Michigan
www.cherrylakepublishing.com

Reading Adviser: Beth Walker Gambro, MS, Ed., Reading Consultant, Yorkville, IL

Photo Credits: © CardIrin/Shutterstock, cover; © Gorodenkoff/Shutterstock, 5; © SritanaN/Shutterstock, 7; © l i g h t p o e t/Shutterstock, 8; © Dima Zel/Shutterstock, 9; © NassornSwitwong/Shutterstock, 11; © Gorodenkoff/Shutterstock, 12; © bbernard/Shutterstock, 13; © lilik ferri yanto/Shutterstock, 14; © Ground Picture/Shutterstock, 15; © Monkey Business Images/Shutterstock, 17; © aslysun/Shutterstock, 18; © SofikoS/Shutterstock, 19; © Ned Snowman/Shutterstock, 21; © Quality Stock Arts/Shutterstock, 22; © Max4e Photo/Shutterstock, 23; © iamlukyeee/Shutterstock, 24; © Orsan Elitok/Shutterstock, 25; © NassornSnitwong/Shutterstock, 27; © MNBB Studio/Shutterstock, 28; © SuperOhMo/Shutterstock, 29; © Gorodenkoff/Shutterstock, 31

Copyright © 2026 by Cherry Lake Publishing Group
All rights reserved. No part of this book may be reproduced or utilized in any form or by any means without written permission from the publisher.

Cherry Lake Press is an imprint of Cherry Lake Publishing Group.

Library of Congress Cataloging-in-Publication Data has been filed and is available at catalog.loc.gov.

Cherry Lake Publishing Group would like to acknowledge the work of the Partnership for 21st Century Learning, a Network of Battelle for Kids. Please visit Battelle for Kids online for more information.

Printed in the United States of America

Note from publisher: Websites change regularly, and their future contents are outside of our control. Supervise children when conducting any recommended online searches for extended learning opportunities.

Diane Lindsey Reeves likes to write books that help students figure out what they want to be when they grow up. She mostly lives in Washington, D.C., but spends as much time as she can in North Carolina and South Carolina with her grandkids.

CONTENTS

Introduction:
In the Know | 4

Chapter 1:
Robotics Engineers Know...How Robots Can Change the Future | 6

Chapter 2:
Robotics Engineers Know... All About Robotics | 10

Chapter 3:
Robotics Engineers Know... The Tools of the Trade | 16

Chapter 4:
Robotics Engineers Know... How to Work Safely | 20

Chapter 5:
Robotics Engineers Know... How to Find the Job They Want | 26

Stop, Think, and Write | 30
Things to Do If You Want to Be a Robotics Engineer | 30
Learn More | 31
Glossary, Index | 32

In the Know

Every career you can imagine has one thing in common: It takes an expert. Career experts need to know more about how to do a specific job than other people do. That's how everyone from plumbers to rocket scientists gets their job done.

Sometimes it takes years of college study to learn what they need to know. Other times, people learn by working alongside someone who is already a career expert. No matter how they learn, it takes a career expert to do any job well.

Take **robotics** engineers, for instance. Today, robots are changing the world as we know it. They are widely used in manufacturing. They are used to run **automated** teller machines (ATMs) at banks. They are used for everything from disposing of bombs to vacuuming floors. And engineers help all of them work.

Robotics engineers are good at:

- **Understanding STEM**
- **Thinking creatively**
- **Designing complex solutions**
- **Learning new things**

CHAPTER 1

Robotics Engineers Know... How Robots Can Change the Future

Robots are machines that can do complex tasks. They may do jobs that are hard for humans to do, like lifting heavy things. They also may do repetitive tasks on assembly lines or dangerous tasks in hard-to-reach places.

Robotics engineers are the humans who teach robots how to behave. They start by identifying a problem they want the robot to solve. For instance, maybe a cookie maker wants to pack boxes more efficiently. A robot could pack packages of cookies into a box for shipping. Robotics engineers would look at how a human would do that task. Then they would design a system to mimic the process. Next they would program the robot to copy each motion. Sound complicated? It is! And an exciting challenge.

Robotic assembly lines were first created in the 1980s.

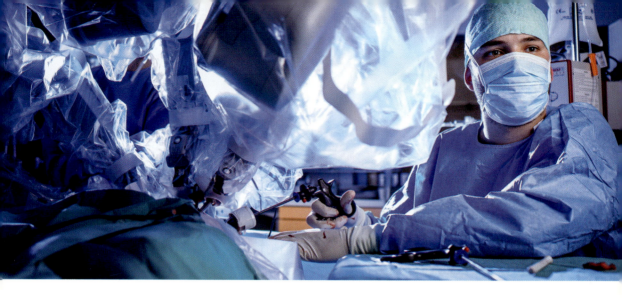

Right now, robots can only assist humans, but in the future, they may be able to do surgery themselves!

Some of the first robots were used in manufacturing. It is safe to say that robots have totally changed the way many products are made. Assembly lines used to be run by humans. Now robots do many of those jobs. In fact, robots often do the jobs better than humans do. They are quicker and more precise. They do not get tired or make mistakes even when doing the same tasks over and over again. Robots are controlled by computers. The computers are controlled by humans.

Now robots are changing the way almost everything is done. In health care, robots help doctors perform surgeries. Tiny nanobots are used to get medicine to hard-to-reach parts of the body. Some robots even zap germs.

Robots are used in exciting ways in many industries. Robots help astronauts with certain tasks aboard the International Space Station. They protect soldiers and defuse bombs in war zones. Robots are used to move products from one place to another in warehouses. Self-driving cars are robots programmed to react to common driving situations.

With new advances in **artificial intelligence** (AI), robotics engineers can design robots that perform tasks faster and more accurately. Be on the lookout to see how even more robots are used to change the way the world works.

ROBOTS ON MARS!

The National Aeronautical and Space Administration (NASA) has sent five robot **rovers** to explore Mars. Their names are *Sojourner*, *Spirit*, *Opportunity*, *Curiosity*, and *Perseverance*. These rovers have made remarkable discoveries about the faraway red planet. They do work that would be impossible for humans to do. NASA hopes that their work will one day make it possible for humans to visit and maybe even live on the planet.

CHAPTER 2

Robotics Engineers Know... All About Robotics

Humans and robots have a lot in common. Humans have a body. They have muscles to move the body. They have senses that receive information about the body and the world around it. They also have a power source to turn on muscles and sensors. Their brains process information and tell the body what to do.

Likewise, a robot has a movable physical structure and some sort of motor to move it. It has sensors and a power supply to turn it off and on. A computer "brain" controls it all. This is one of the first things a robotics engineer needs to know. Everything they do is based on the understanding that robots are meant to be human copycats.

A robot's "brain" is made up of sensors and controls that send signals to the "body" and tell it what to do.

11

AI is new and still unknown. Part of a robotic engineer's job is to experiment with this new technology.

It sounds simple, but knowing and doing are two different things. Strong skills in math, science, and technology are essential. Robotics engineers apply science, technology, engineering, and math (STEM) knowledge to problems, resulting in amazing solutions.

Robotics engineers also need to know about artificial intelligence (AI). AI is moving robotics forward in bold new ways. So far, robotics has focused on teaching robots how to perform tasks like humans. The robotics engineer does the thinking and programs the robot to do a specific task in a specific way. AI has the potential to learn how to think like humans itself.

Robotics engineers work in teams. They collaborate to solve complex problems and innovate.

AI has many unique uses, such as writing code and reading complex text. Robotics engineers can use it to speed up these tasks.

The goal of AI is to learn to do things that require human intelligence. This includes learning, reasoning, problem-solving, and understanding language. True AI does not exist yet. What we call "AI" today are complex **language models**.

AI requires powerful computers, complex **algorithms**, and enormous amounts of data to achieve its results. The biggest challenge is using it in **ethical** ways that protect people and the planet.

AI IN YOUR POCKET?

Are people carrying artificial intelligence around in their smartphones? If it is an Apple phone, it may have a program called Siri. If it is an Android phone, it may have a program called Google Assistant. These voice assistants answer questions, play music, make phone calls, and do all kinds of helpful tasks. They are excellent examples of existing technology. You talk. They listen. And then they talk back! But they don't think. They are just complex programs.

CHAPTER 3

Robotics Engineers Know... The Tools of the Trade

Brain power is one of the most important tools in a robotics engineer's toolbox. It takes a combination of electrical, mechanical, and computer engineering skills to create a useful robot. Robotics engineers get serious about STEM learning. They need at least a college bachelor's degree to do what they do.

Along with technical skills, robotics engineers need plenty of curiosity and imagination. These skills help them design creative solutions to all kinds of problems. Robotics engineers are good at thinking outside of the box to come up with original solutions.

Learning about engineering doesn't have to start in college. Try joining a STEM club at school.

Robotics engineers write computer code to control the behavior and motions of robots. They use programming languages such as C++ and Python, as well as specialized robot operating systems (ROS) to program robots to do specific tasks. Computer-aided design (CAD) software lets them design and **simulate** what a robot will look like before it is built. Engineers use these tools to test robot designs and behaviors before they build actual **prototypes**. This process saves time and money. It also lets them work out the kinks online before going live.

MACHINE OR ROBOT?

What's the difference between a machine and a robot?

The answer is how much human help it needs. Machines need human intervention. Robots are programmed to work on their own. One example is vacuum cleaners. A regular vacuum cleaner has a handle. It takes a human pushing it around to get it to work. Robotic vacuums are programmed with sensors to tell them where to go and what to do. Just click a button and—*presto!*—clean floors.

When building robot prototypes, robotics engineers use tools you may have lying around your house.

AI is currently used by these engineers for two things. It can copy an action. It can also perform rapid data analysis. AI has the potential to do more things in the future—things that have never been possible before. Caution is advised!

There are times when robotics engineers need to reach into a more traditional toolbox. They may need to adjust things when building robot prototypes. That's when tools like screwdrivers, pliers, wire cutters, and wrenches come in handy.

CHAPTER 4

Robotics Engineers Know... How to Work Safely

Isaac Asimov was not a robotics engineer. He was a science fiction writer who wrote about robots. It is especially interesting that he wrote about robots before real robots were invented. He had a vivid imagination and could see a future where robotics could be used for good or evil.

Perhaps this is why Asimov came up with three laws for robots in 1942. First, he said that a robot may not injure a human or allow a human to be injured by not taking action. Second, a robot must obey orders given to it by humans. This was true as long as the orders did not break the first law. The third law was that a robot must protect its own existence as long as it doesn't conflict with the first or second laws.

Robots are already interacting with humans more than ever before. There are entire robot-run restaurants and cafes. The robots in these places obey orders given by humans.

When working with large machinery, robotics engineers may wear goggles and headphones to protect themselves.

The idea of robot laws is interesting, but robots will do as they are programmed. They are already used in war and combat. They can already be used for harm. It is people who must decide how robotics should be used. There is so much potential to use it for the good of humanity. But there is a danger that some could misuse it.

Besides rules about ethical use, robotics engineers must also follow rules to stay physically safe. Some rules are simple, like keeping hair secure and not wearing loose clothing or jewelry. Other rules get more complicated. After all, they are working with powerful technology. An out-of-control robot is the last thing a robotics engineer wants to deal with.

ROBOTIC LIMBS

Sometimes people lose an arm, leg, or hand due to injury or disease. A **prosthesis** is an artificial device used to replace a missing body part. For a long time, the devices used to replace limbs were clunky and difficult to use. New robotic devices now connect with a person's mind *and* body. They mimic natural functions in amazing ways. People with prostheses are running marathons, playing sports, and living active lives.

After graduating college, robotics engineers often spend several months under the guidance of an experienced engineer.

Emergency stop buttons help protect against robotic malfunctions and software glitches that can be dangerous.

That's why engineers spend a lot of effort preventing problems before they happen. They pay close attention to creating safe workplaces. They make sure to put emergency stop buttons and other safety measures in place. They also devote a lot of energy to training employees to work safely.

CHAPTER 5

Robotics Engineers Know... How to Find the Job They Want

Are you thinking about a career in robotics? If so, you have some important choices to make. These choices will determine how much education you need to pursue. They will allow you to work on projects that match your interests. And they will help you focus your talents in useful ways.

It is possible to get started as a robotics technician with just a high school diploma. However, many employers prefer to hire techs who have completed a 2-year engineering program at a community college or technical school. Robotics technicians help robotics engineers develop, operate, and test robotic systems and machines. It can be a great way to get into the field and explore more options.

Robotics technicians troubleshoot issues and assist engineers in any way they can.

Robotics engineers need at least a bachelor's degree in computer science or engineering. The more education and experience they have, the more opportunities are available to them. Popular majors include mechanical, electrical, and computer engineering. Robotics engineering degrees are also an option at some schools. Deciding which educational path to pursue is the first big choice for robotics engineers.

Choosing which industry to work in is another exciting choice for robotics professionals. Do they want to work in manufacturing or health care? Are they interested in aerospace or transportation? Maybe they'd prefer to work on agricultural or food-related projects. Defense is an area of interest for others. Opportunities await in all of these industries and more!

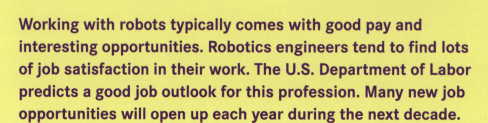

HELP WANTED

Working with robots typically comes with good pay and interesting opportunities. Robotics engineers tend to find lots of job satisfaction in their work. The U.S. Department of Labor predicts a good job outlook for this profession. Many new job opportunities will open up each year during the next decade.

Writing code is an awesome way to get involved in engineering. There are even camps for kids like you to learn code!

Robotics engineers also choose how to use their engineering skills. Are they experts in writing software code? Do they want to develop the hardware and circuits that run robotic systems? Maybe they excel in designing interfaces that help people communicate with robots. That's what user interface (UI) and user experience (UX) designers do. There are many special areas where robotics engineers can let their skills shine.

Activity

Stop, Think, and Write

Can you imagine a world without robotics engineers? How do they make the places we live, work, and play better?

Get a separate sheet of paper. On one side, answer this question:

- *How do robotics engineers make the world a better place?*

On the other side of the paper:

- *Draw a picture of a robot you designed that can clean your room.*

Things to Do If You Want to Be a Robotics Engineer

Interested in working with robots? There are things you can do now and later to figure out if being a robotics engineer is a good career fit for you.

NOW

- Take lots of science, math, and technology classes.
- Use LEGOS® to design your own robot.
- Sign up for a robotics or engineering camp program.
- Get involved in an Odyssey of the Mind or other similar competition at your school.

LATER

- Keep up with the latest innovations in robotic and AI software.
- Be prepared to work hard and study complex subject matter.
- Earn at least a bachelor's degree in robotics or engineering.

Learn More

Books

Gregory, Josh. *AI in the Workplace.* Ann Arbor, MI: Cherry Lake, 2025.

Gregory, Josh. *Careers in Robot Technology.* Ann Arbor, MI: Cherry Lake, 2018.

Maslyk, Jacie. *The Fascinating Engineering Book for Kids.* Emeryville, CA: Rockridge Press, 2021.

Newland, Sonya. *Working with Computers and Robots.* Tulsa, OK: Kane Miller, 2022.

On the Web

With an adult, learn more online with these suggested searches.

Kiddle — Robotics Facts for Kids

NASA — Robotics for Kids

PBS Learning Media — Robotics in Medicine — Video

31

Glossary

algorithms (AL-guh-rih-thuhmz) processes or sets of rules to be followed in calculations or problem-solving operations

artificial intelligence (ar-tuh-FIH-shuhl in-TEH-luh-juhns) computers and machines that can reason, learn, and act in ways that mimic human intelligence

automated (AH-tuh-may-tuhd) carried out by machines or computers without human labor

ethical (EH-thih-kuhl) related to good and honest morals

language models (LANG-gwij MAH-duhls) complex computer programs that analyze and predict word patterns

nanobots (NAA-noh-bahts) microscopically small robots

prosthesis (prahs-THEE-suhs) artificial device that replaces a human body part

prototypes (PROH-tuh-tiyps) first versions of a product

robotics (roh-BAH-tiks) science of designing, making, and using robots

rovers (ROH-vuhrz) vehicles that can explore places in outer space

simulate (SIM-yuh-layt) to mimic or imitate something

STEM (STEM) science, technology, engineering, and math

Index

activities, 30
artificial intelligence (AI), 9, 12, 14–15, 19–20, 22
Asimov, Isaac, 20
assembly lines, 6–8
automation of tasks, 4, 6–9

coding, 14, 18, 29

education, 4–5, 12, 16–17, 24, 26, 28, 30
ethics with AI, 15, 19, 20, 22

job market, 28

language models, 14

manufacturing technologies, 4, 6–8
Mars, 9

problem-solving, 6, 12–14, 16, 25
programming, 14, 18, 29
prostheses, 23

robotic limbs, 23
robotics engineers
  job descriptions, 6, 8–9, 12, 18, 26–29
  skills, 5, 12, 16
  tools, 16–19
robotics technicians, 26–27
robots
  engineering processes, 6, 8–12, 16, 18–19, 23, 30
  laws for, 20, 22
  structures, 10–11
  types and jobs, 4, 6–9, 13, 18

safety, 20–25
smartphones, 15
space missions, 9
STEM fields, 5, 12, 16
study and training, 4–5, 12, 16–17, 24, 26, 28, 30

technicians, 26–27

UI and UX designers, 29

virtual assistants, 15